I0060102

Praise for *5 Steps to Get You...* and *Ready to Go When You Are*

"I love the book. It is a good, quick, informative read for people who want to sell their business. Thank you for sharing."

JAKE FACKRELL, SERIAL ENTREPRENEUR AND CEO OF USHC HOLDINGS, INC.

"Your words are eloquent, thought provoking and absolutely on point. You have captured the components of why people fail or succeed. I believe this book should be given to every loan officer who helps a company secure a loan in the process of starting or growing a business."

MAXINE ROSEN, INVESTMENT AND FINANCIAL ADVISOR

"Easy read. Love the quick tips at the end of each chapter. Great tool and guide for small business owners."

RONNELL T. SPEARS, CIO OF HOME CARE BY BLACK STONE

"I really enjoyed the book and there are many valuable ideas for the business owners who would never consider themselves sellers. I appreciated the Prioritizing chapter and the Systemizing chapter is fabulous. You have good focus and I see how many aspects of the book could benefit our company. I plan to use your ideas. I like the fact you are an apparent commoner who along the way held on to your compassion, family and faith. My hat's off to you."

VINCENT HULL, ENTREPRENEUR AND PRESIDENT OF SELECT HOME CARE

"The book is brilliant. Excellent advice. As a small business owner, I know we typically do not plan for our eventual exit. Want to know what you don't know? Read the book!"

CHERYL SMITH-RIZK, BUSINESS OWNER AND CONSULTANT

"Great job! And great resource for all new and current business owners."

GINNY KENYON, OWNER KENYON HOME CARE CONSULTING

5 STEPS TO GET YOUR BUSINESS FIT
and ready to go when you are

5 STEPS to GET YOUR BUSINESS FIT

and ready to go when you are

RISA BAKER

PARTNERS 31, LLC
Atlanta

5 Steps to Get Your Business Fit and Ready to Go When You Are

© 2014 by Risa Baker

All rights are reserved. No part of this publication may be reproduced in any form or by any electronic or mechanical means, including information storage and retrieval systems, without permission in writing by the publisher, except by a reviewer who may quote brief passages in a review. For information regarding permission, contact the author at risa@risabaker.com

DISCLAIMER: This publication is designed to provide information about the subject matter covered. It is with the sole understanding that neither the author nor the publisher is engaged by the reader to render brokerage, legal, financial, investment, accounting, or other professional services. The purpose of this book is to educate. The author or the publisher shall have no liability or responsibility to any person or entity with respect to any loss or damage caused or alleged to be caused directly or indirectly by the information contained in this book.

Published by Partners31, LLC
www.Partners31.com
Atlanta, Georgia

Cover & Interior Design by Imagine! Studios, LLC
www.ArtsImagine.com

ISBN: 978-0-9895874-0-2
LCCN: 2014902501

First Partners31, LLC printing: March 2014

To my Dad, Richard A. Ward,
and entrepreneurs and business owners everywhere
who dare to make a difference by sharing your dreams,
talents and experiences.

TABLE OF CONTENTS

Introduction 11

Where to Start: Three No's to Know 15

1. Organizing 27

2. Customizing 35

3. Systemizing 43

4. Prioritizing 55

5. Analyzing 65

Conclusion 75

Fit Tips Summary Guide 79

About the Author 83

INTRODUCTION

"You cannot open a book without
learning something."

CONFUCIUS

Did you know that, according to Deloitte & Touche, 71 percent of small and mid-size business owners plan to exit their business within the next 10 years? It probably has something to do with the silver tsunami, aka baby boomers. But just because an owner wants to sell the business does not mean that the business is actually going to sell. At any time, approximately 20 percent of businesses are for sale—but only one out of five actually sells. Why is that?

According to the Small Business Association, the primary cause for failure is (can you believe it?) *lack of planning!*

Most business owners start with the idea of dedicating 110% of their time and talent to having a great and successful company. ***Planning for the unexpected requires focus***

on being prepared, open and ready to take advantage of the future. If you decide to sell or receive an unsolicited offer from a buyer, you will want as much for the business as possible.

But the challenge is that few organizations genuinely understand how to reach those goals.

Other alarming facts revealed in a recent study by Harris Interactive found that 66% of small and mid-size business owners do NOT have an exit plan. With business failures increasing, and close to 95 percent of start-up businesses closing within five years, it might be time to address the "lack of planning" issue.

There is always a market for FIT, healthy businesses. Buyers look for businesses that are sustainable and have good growth, low risk and high returns—the same things you would like to see in your business.

Acknowledge that sooner or later you are going to leave your business. You might not be ready to exit today. It might not be for five or ten years down the road, but you *must* plan ahead in order to exit on *your* terms.

The goal of this book is to motivate you to build a business that is *FIT and ready to go when you are.* A business with a *plan*, a business with great *people* and a business with solid *profit* is a company that is increasing value and decreasing risk—a FIT company! In this book I will share with you the key components of getting your business FIT—the importance of organizing, customizing, systemizing, prioritizing and analyzing.

When you determine your best option for leaving your business, whether selling or transferring to employees, partners or family members, execute your plan with determination and control.

Identifying the business goals that are most important to you will help ensure they are met. Nothing can be worse than for an owner to say, "OK, we're ready to move forward and sell," only to discover after all the years of hard work, some very real obstacles prevent a desirable transition. Simply put, getting your business FIT is an intentional and deliberate approach for identifying your objectives so you can leave it with your goals met.

The goal of planning ahead is to focus on your objectives. Create a plan as early as possible and then stick to that plan as long as you maintain your business.

Start now—Get Your Business FIT and ready to go when you are!

FIT TIPS

1 Planning for the unexpected requires focus on being prepared, open and ready to take advantage of the future.

2 There is always a market for FIT, healthy businesses.

3 Planning ahead and identifying the things that are most important to you will help ensure your objectives are met.

4 The goal of planning ahead is to identify and focus on your objectives.

WHERE TO START:
THREE NO'S TO KNOW
avoid these mistakes

> *"I am certainly not one of those who need to be prodded. In fact, if anything, I am the prod."*
>
> WINSTON CHURCHILL

Owning and running a business is hard work. And you want *your* energy and labor focused on growing a healthy business, not an unhealthy one.

The goal is to increase value and decrease risk. But there are three mistakes you could be making that yield the exact opposite. I have worked with countless business owners over the years. I hate it when I'm asked to analyze their business and find they have made one or all of these mistakes—actually creating higher risk and decreasing the value of the business.

Did you ever wonder why one business has buyers lined up willing to pay top dollar while another sits on the market for months or years? A buyer's willingness to pay a premium price centers on his perception of risk and return. When targeting acquisitions for a large corporation, I met with many owners who had the fairy tale notion that one day a buyer would contact them, negotiate a sale (at a premium price, of course), and they would live happily ever after. But that was not the case with most companies. More often than not, a sale could not be negotiated and the elusive "happily ever after" was foiled.

Hopefully, you enjoy your business and are in no hurry to sell. But, again, it is HARD work and you should want to grow the most FIT and healthy business you can. Why spend your time growing an unhealthy one?

Where do you start? Recognize these three costly *(and I do mean costly)* mistakes and take steps to avoid them:

- No Plan
- No People
- No Profit

MISTAKE #1—NO PLAN

Consider these questions:

- Have you decided how much longer you want to work in your business?

- Do you know how much profit you will need from the sale of the business?
- What is your business worth today?
- Have you chosen your exit path or have a successor in mind?
- Do you have a plan for your business if something unexpected happens to you?

Would any of these responses be yours?

- I have no idea when I want to exit.
- I have not determined how much money I'll need for the sale of my business.
- I don't know the value of my company.
- I haven't decided what I ultimately want to do with my business.
- I don't want to exit right now so I don't need a plan, and besides, I'm healthy.

Many business owners are either overwhelmed by the thought of leaving or are so busy fighting daily fires they think they cannot plan their exits—the classic "I don't have time!" But know this—indecision is the wrong decision. Winston Churchill once said, "I never worry about action, but only about inaction." The irrefutable fact is, one day you will leave your business. *Passively choosing no plan is a decision to settle for the least profitable exit for yourself and your family.*

Planning takes time. Preparing to get your business FIT and completing a top dollar transaction takes three to five years, on average. More time typically reduces risk—time used to design and implement tax-saving strategies, build value and strengthen your management team. In a competitive market, only the best-prepared, FIT businesses sell for top dollar. And the owners of those FIT businesses will be those who made the decision to plan and prepare years ahead of the actual sale.

THE NO PLAN COMPANY
(Increased Risk and Decreased Value)

A few years ago I was working with an owner who was very interested in selling, and we began gathering data and information for analysis of the last three years of operation. I will refer to this company as the NO PLAN Company.

Analysis year 1, the business had approximately $15 million in revenue. The profit for that year was $1.2 million or 8 percent of revenue—a little low. The revenue was good. The owner made a good salary and enjoyed a very comfortable lifestyle.

Year 2 analysis reflected a slight increase in revenue to $15.8 million, but a downtrend in profit from the $1.2 million the previous year to $990,000 (a $210,000 profit decrease). Revenue of $15.8 million was slightly up but profit moved from 8 percent to 6.3 percent. Red flag is waving!

The current year reflected a decrease in revenue from $15.8 million to $15.2 million, and profit dollars fell from $990,000 to $980,000—wrong direction for sure. Now we hear the warning sirens screaming DANGER, DANGER.

On this decreasing revenue and decreasing profit information alone, company value declined well over $1 million during these three years. Year 1 valuation would have been approximately $4 million to $4.5 million. The current year fair market valuation would be right at $3 million on the low end to *maybe* $3.5 million on the high end.

As we continued our analysis, the problems resulting from a lack of planning became daunting. The owner was approaching 70 and assumed he would be able to sell his company at will. He also had not told his accountant he wanted to sell. He had chosen to set up the company as a C Corporation, and the corporation owned real estate. Problem: The owner did not want to sell the real estate. No pre-tax planning had been done. The negative tax ramifications of such a sale had never been discussed between the owner and his accountant. Now, with the C Corporation structure, negative tax issues would surface no matter what option he chose regarding the real estate and the sale.

With the decline in business value and the impending tax obligations, he decided he could not sell as he had hoped. No plan and no sale.

THE COMPANY WITH A PLAN
(Decreased Risk, Increased Value)

Now let's review a company with a *plan*, whose owners from Day 1 planned to build the company and eventually sell it. In our three-year review of this business, year 1 revenue was $5 million with a 20 percent profit margin, or $1 million. Not bad.

Year 2 brought $5.5 million in revenue and a slight decrease in profit dollars, down from $1 million to $988,000. In this year the owners were bolstering their processes and procedures, creating a solid infrastructure and sales team.

Year 3 saw an increase in revenue and profit—total of $7 million in sales and $1.3 million in profit.

The owners were working their plan to grow and had definitely lowered risk and increased value. The company sold for double the value of the no plan company.

Think about it. If I were to ask you which company you would consider to be worth more—a company doing $15 million in business or a company doing $7 million in business, which would be the logical choice? You would think the larger company doing $15 million in sales. How can it be that a company doing more than double the sales was valued at nearly half the price?

This is a glaring comparison between growing a large company and growing a valuable company.

In his book *The One Thing You Need To Know*, Marcus Buckingham writes, "As a leader, you are never satisfied with the present, because in your head you can see a better future, and the friction between what is and what could be burns you, stirs you up, propels you forward."

The difference between these two companies was planning—tackling the "friction" between the "what is" and "what could be." One chose to settle into comfort and convenience. The other continued to battle and press toward the "what could be."

Are you ready to operate in the "what could be?" Set your goal to correct the no-plan mistake. Identify your objectives, know where you stand today, and choose your desired exit path.

Failing to plan for your exit means you run the risk of being forced to sell your company because of unexpected events, poor economic conditions, poor management decisions, bankruptcy or other disastrous events. Liquidating the business because of declining sales or losing more than 50 percent of sale proceeds because of poor tax planning are other unhappy endings that result from no planning or poor planning.

If leaving a company you've worked so hard to build and having little or nothing to show for it is unacceptable to you, please start now. Get a plan in place!

Decide and plan accordingly. Take the following steps:

- Fix a departure date—Know how much longer you want to work in the business.
- Determine your financial needs—If the sale of your business is your retirement nest egg, know your required after-tax income.
- Decide on a successor—outside party or inside transfer to co-owner, family member or key employee.
- Know the market value of your business today— Value is critical to determine whether your financial objectives can be met at present or if value must increase in order to reach your objectives.

Decide now to create the best possible exit path. Failure to act can potentially be fatal to a successful exit. The decision is simply too important to leave to chance.

MISTAKE #2—NO PEOPLE

Many owners are surprised to discover their company's worth is less than expected. Two main reasons are lack of business systems or lack a strong management team. All the company value is tied up in its owner's presence.

But people are your most valuable asset! *One of the most important value drivers in any business is its management team.*

You need a team with talent and staying power. *One of the first questions a prospective buyer will ask is, "Who runs the company and are they willing to stay?"* If the answer is "The owner and he does not wish to stay," the value plummets and most buyers will look elsewhere.

Good management teams are so valuable because they are difficult to assemble and even more difficult to keep together! A solid management team in place equates to continued success with customers and employees, thereby ensuring stability in the business—decreasing risk and increasing value. When you face tough times, having people who possess the capacity to turn things around is imperative. Your best chance of renewed success comes from a great team that understands challenge, has faced difficulties before and has experience making the tough decisions. If your business is dependent upon your (or any one person's) personal relationships and reputation alone, you are the management "team." Risk goes up and value goes down.

To address this issue, one owner diverted a portion of profits into adopting more formal systems and processes, and into building a management team that could replace him following his retirement. By making less money over the short term, he succeeded in increasing his value *(and decreasing his risk)* over time.

Another owner began attending retirement seminars when he was 28. Today he is the CEO of the family business. He is following his father's footsteps to make proactive plans to transition ownership to a new leader. His objective for success is to have delegated 100 percent of his job responsibilities by the time he is 60.

Jake is the man with a plan. "When building a team, I would take on a position and build it up," he says. "Then I would hire someone that could fill the role. I would step out and work more on the business. We would grow more and then we would bring someone else on, continuing to add infrastructure and horsepower to keep it running."

In many instances, the owner bottlenecks the company. You have to be able to get out of the way and let the company run. Empower your people to run as well. If you have to make every single decision, you are not building a FIT business and you are limiting yourself. Be smart enough to hire smarter people!

MISTAKE #3—NO PROFIT

You cannot ask too many questions about your financials. No question is off limits when it comes to this area of your business. Ask who, what, where, when, why, how. And make sure you get answers. You need to track sales, hours, billing and billing cycles, pay rates, billing rates, overtime hours, referrals, incoming phone calls, time of day you receive the most calls, sales closures. I think you get the picture.

I worked with a company several years ago whose owners had a spreadsheet tracking 15 years worth of referral sources—who they were, how many clients came from each source and when. That is an example of meaningful tracking—and with that level of detail you can see specific trending. Is

December typically a good month? Does business slack off in the summer months? When fall comes, do sales increase?

This may come as a surprise, but you or someone on your team needs to explain financial parameters and relevance to each team member. I once ran an operation that provided Medicaid services to people 24 hours a day, 7 days a week. When I came on board it was a mess! There were turnover problems with staff, account receivables were in disarray, billing problems abounded, overtime pay was gigantic and service quality was insufficient. Problems, problems, problems, mess, mess, mess!

What I discovered in the turnaround process was that those responsible for the paperwork and authorization for payment process had a huge disconnect with those who were responsible for billing.

I started having meetings with everyone involved to close the lack-of-understanding gap. I explained to the team that if paperwork was not current and submitted correctly, we could not bill for the services we had provided. Therefore we would not get paid. If we wanted to stay in business, and everyone agreed we did, we could not provide our services for free. Problem solved!

Don't assume your staff understands the business as you do. Communicate and teach them what they need to know about the financial pieces of the business.

This is what it takes on a daily basis to keep your business profitable, healthy and growing. It's not a commitment to sell. It's a commitment to get your business FIT. Get it to a place where you have the option to sell should the right opportunity come along.

As we dive into *Get Your Business FIT*, you will be fully aware of these costly mistakes—No Plan, No People, No Profit—and how to avoid having them become a part of your business.

FIT TIPS

1   **The goal is to increase value and decrease risk.**

2   **Passively choosing *no plan* is a decision to settle for the *least* profitable exit for yourself and your family.**

3   **One of the most important value drivers in any business is its management team.**

4   **One of the first questions a prospective buyer will ask is, "Who runs the company and are they willing to stay?**

5   **Don't assume your staff understands the business as you do.**

1 ORGANIZING
Structures, Setups and Shares

"There are no secrets to success. It is the result of preparation, hard work and learning from failure."

COLIN POWELL

Whether you are planning to start a business or have been in business many years, have a defined exit objective. Consider your options: selling to an outside third party, some type of inside transaction such as selling to a partner or employee(s), or making your business a gift to your children. For companies of a certain size, perhaps an employee stock option plan would be a good option. Of course, liquidation and bankruptcy are options as well, but not good ones.

How you organize your business is an extremely important piece of your FITness plan. Defining your exit objective on the front end should guide your choice of entity structure.

Your goal is to hedge your risk, and planning ahead enables you to achieve that goal.

ENTITY STRUCTURE

In working with hundreds of business owners over the past decade, I've seen all kinds of surprising things. Your choice of business structure may seem unimportant or elementary, but I assure you it is not!

Whether you have a start-up or an established business, *it is important to know and understand your entity structure.* Is your business set up as a C Corporation, an S Corporation, an LLC (limited liability corporation), or Sole Proprietorship? Organizing this one item can cost or save you money.

I am not an accountant or an attorney, but my experience with selling or not selling companies has proven how vitally important it is to choose the right entity structure. Please meet with your team of advisors and ask questions about your entity structure and make certain you are comfortable with the answers. Share information about your future successor plans with your advisors. Ask if other entity options would work better for you.

I have a friend and previous client who set up her business 20 years ago as a C Corporation. I told her that if she intended to sell the business at some point, there would be a limited pool of buyers who would be willing to do a stock purchase for her small business. And if she did an asset sale, she would have adverse tax ramifications.

Did you know that if your business is structured as a Sole Proprietorship your personal assets could be at risk? Did you know that if you set up in the beginning as a C Corporation and then decide to change to an S Corporation there is a 10-year look-back that could mean potential tax consequences?

Taxes are a fact of life. And let's face it, a huge expense. It takes pre-planning to save as much as you can. Do what you can within the confines of the law. Be smart about it.

I am not suggesting there is only one *right* way. But you do need to know the best structure for you and your business. Also, understand that it can change over the years. So ask questions of your accountant, legal advisors and yourself to define your exit objective so that you can plan accordingly.

ADVISOR TEAM

None of us is an expert in every area. Please know your strengths and weaknesses and form your team of advisors based on your needs. You may be the visionary, the manager or the technician (as suggested in Michael Gerber's book *The E-Myth Revisited*). It is not likely that you will be all three. Technical proficiency does *not* guarantee financial success. The key to a successful business is business skills and tools. If you don't have all the tools, get help.

Ensure you are investing in yourself and your business! Make time to work *on* the business, not just *for* the business. Take advantage of learning and education to keep your business and yourself moving forward. Remember, you can't give what you don't have to give.

BUY-SELL AGREEMENT

If you currently have partners and you* do not *have a buy-sell agreement, PLEASE, PLEASE GET ONE. It is a legally binding agreement that gives guidance and governs handling of ownership shares in the event of co-owner death, divorce or disability, or if a co-owner is forced or chooses to leave the business. It is best to draft the agreement on the front end, when everyone is calm and getting along.

Buy-sell agreements are between business partners and shareholders and consist of several legally binding clauses. The agreement controls:

- Who can buy a departing partner's shares.
- What events will trigger a buyout (the most common being death, disability, retirement or owner leaving).
- What price will be paid for the ownership interest.

Business partners had better have one!

A buy-sell agreement makes sense for *any* business with partners, no matter what the entity structure. You can have a buy-sell agreement with two owners or many.

For example, you and your partner Sam run a lawn business. Sam dies. Do you still own the business? Is Sam's wife or child your new partner? Do you have the right or obligation to buy them out? If so, for how much? What terms? What if you die first? What happens if one of you becomes disabled or files bankruptcy?

Turmoil and confusion rule without a buy-sell agreement in place. No matter what the size of the business, these potential issues among partners are easy to prevent with a buy-sell in place, but expensive otherwise. Seek assistance from a business or tax lawyer experienced in buy-sell agreements. The initial expense will be nothing compared to what it can save you!

It may be difficult to address these issues, but are you willing to face the risk created by not having an agreement in place? One of the beauties of the buy-sell agreement is that it makes the process of negotiating and agreeing on terms for triggering events easier than you might think.

And while we are on the topic of partnerships, I would like to mention one other tip for FITness: *Avoid setting up partnerships with all partners having equal shares.* Someone should have majority ownership to fend off stagnation and other issues that arise in the business life cycle.

I met with a couple who owned a business with two other owners. They had set up the partnership 10 years before with equal ownership between the four of them at 25 percent each. Now the partnership was no longer working.

They had no one with majority ownership to be the "tie-breaker" in any disputes. More importantly, they had not created a buy-sell agreement when the partnership began. They had no legal document with set rules for buying or selling each other's shares of ownership, no base for valuation of the business. *Not* a good situation!

This is just one story of many I could share. If you have a buy-sell agreement in place, *when was the last time you and your partners reviewed it?* This is a big deal. Keep the agreement current! ***I recommend reviewing the buy-sell agreement at least once per year.***

WHAT'S IN A NAME?

One final thought—what's in a name? The name of your business makes a significant difference. As I was jogging one morning I passed a parked vehicle. On the side was a sign advertising "Broken Dreams Lawn Care." The multi-rust-colored dilapidated truck served as additional branding. I smiled to myself as I jogged past.

The rest of my morning outing I kept thinking to myself, "I definitely would *not* call that business to do my lawn service!" Would you? The name just does not give those warm fuzzy I-just-have-to-do-business-with-you feelings. My consumer brain kicked in and I began imagining what it might look like to have Broken Dreams Lawn Care do my lawn maintenance. It was not pretty.

Suffice it to say, the name you choose for your business matters.

FIT TIPS

1 Know and understand your entity structure.

2 If you currently have partners and you do not have a buy-sell agreement, *please, please get one.*

3 Avoid setting up partnerships with all partners having equal shares.

4 Review the buy-sell agreement at least once per year.

2 CUSTOMIZING
Best, Good, Rethink

> *"There is only one boss. The customer. And he can
> fire everybody in the company from the chairman on
> down, simply by spending his money somewhere else."*
>
> SAM WALTON

I was with my husband the other day picking up new eye-glasses. I asked if I could make my next appointment. I was told the people who made appointments were not located in that office area. To make an appointment I had to call the other office.

I did see a sign on the front desk that said "Employee in Training," so I am not sure if that truly was the policy or the person behind the desk just didn't know how to make an appointment.

It seems hard to believe that the eye center could not make an appointment for me while I was on site. A thought crossed my mind: Is customer service about the customer or the company?

Of course, we all know what the answer should be. However, companies often implement procedures that seem best for them rather than looking at the situation from the customer's point of view.

Granted, sometimes as customers we don't know what we want or need. But as a business owner, you have the opportunity to form or transform customer perspectives and help them realize your service or product is, as the The Cars sang in 1978, "just what I needed." When did you realize you needed an iPod or a Starbucks latte?

How do you customize your business, focusing on what you do best and what your customers want? Answer: ***Know what you do best as a business***. No business can do everything and be the best at it. Every company has a personality and a culture. It is vital to know where your company excels and capitalize on it. The goal is to know what service or product you provide that meets your customer's needs. Then make excellence, not mediocrity, the standard. ***Customer focus is key***.

How do you know if your customers have a need that is not being met? One way is by making sure every desk with a phone has a call log on it. These logs will start to reveal trends for requests. That's how one company developed a specialty program. If they received requests for a service not currently offered, they would respond, "I'm sorry, we don't do that."

"I'm sorry we don't do that" became a phrase employees were *never* allowed to say. It was a customer service issue. So they revisited customer service and all agreed *"I'm sorry we don't do that"* was not an acceptable response and had to go. With their refocused customer mindset, the new and improved response became, "We don't currently offer that particular service, but here are the names of three people or companies who do. If none of them work out, please call back. We'll do everything we can to help you get what you need."

By intentionally tracking and listening to what customers are asking, you might consider starting a new program and business line! The phone log at the desk is to help you watch for trends. Review it at least monthly. What are people asking for that you are not offering? Then ask, "Is this a service or product we should or could be providing?"

If the answer is "yes," start your research and analysis. If "no," then stay focused on what you do best. Maintain the call logs for other opportunities that might surface.

In most industries, change is a constant. It's important to have learning opportunities to navigate through the change. If you do it right and if your people are on top of these changes, you will discover how to thrive, not just survive— with phenomenal outcomes.

You have identified what you do best. Now, how do you thrive, not just survive? Leverage what you do best. What services would complement your current offerings? Are you open to building additional lines of business? What are the barriers? Are they many or few? How do you respond to requests for services you don't provide?

Have you considered specialty services? For example, if you work with diabetic populations, you might consider providing foot care. Perhaps you could offer home modifications for the disabled in addition to contractor services or as an additional home care or home maintenance service. What about a mom and baby care program? This would work well in an area with young, financially capable, family demographics. Obviously this service would not work so well in a retirement area. A thorough demographic review should be performed to see whether there is customer need *and* financial support for such a business line.

A concierge service for day surgery support could be a good option for certain demographic and geographic areas—a targeted, elite program. With the increase of our aging population, there is opportunity for cruise companions, holiday helpers, skilled and unskilled nursing services.

The list goes on. It's about knowing what you do best, and, if you decide to diversify, what that would look like.

If your business is in the home health arena and located in an area with large companies that require pre-employment health screenings, could that be a diversification of revenue and customization opportunity? What about underwriting exams for insurance companies? Or care management, case management or helping with clinical trials if you are near a medically focused university.

Avoid increasing business risk by having all your eggs in one basket—translation, you need to strive to have multiple payer sources and multiple business lines and revenue sources.

Remember, you won't be able to do everything well and you should *not* offer everything! Never!! Think of targeted possibilities, and then do your homework. Ask yourself, do the demographics support the service? Is there sufficient demand? I am aware of one company that overextended itself in its attempts to customize. The result was that nothing was successful.

A good recommendation is that no more than one additional new service or product be introduced in a year. You want to make sure you can manage it and do it right. Special offerings require special training. There will be education both internally and externally.

Ask yourself each time, "How can I make this the best? What will implementation, training, ongoing training and oversight cost? Are there state rules and regulations affecting what I am trying to offer?"

Do your research. *And never forget what you do best.* Remember, new services and products take time to develop. You will need to implement systems for training, hiring, marketing and sales.

Be creative in how you think and about what you are going to offer. Know your target audience. And consider your profit margins.

- Will it render high demand and high margins? Considered BEST.
- Will it render small demand but high margins? Considered GOOD.
- But if it's small demand and small margins, RETHINK.

No matter how in love you may be with the concept, if it doesn't "pencil," it won't work. You can't change that. You can have the best widget in the world, but if no one wants to buy it, it's not going to sell. Start with the basics—your research, data, facts and demographic review. Is there potential income to support your venture?

As the world continues to change, opportunities abound. You can view change with excitement or with dread. Sitting on the sidelines and waiting to see what the changes will be, will most likely yield missed opportunities.

Create your future. ***Plan to be successful!*** Make sure new ventures are worth your time, money and energy.

Know what you do best and customize your business from that perspective. Don't be afraid to get outside coaching. Build your team of advisors. Build your employees to be a team that listens to your customers and comes to you asking, "We've had nine requests for this in the last two-and-a-half months. Do you think it's something we ought to consider doing?" ***Customizing the business involves every team member's efforts and ideas.***

FIT TIPS

1 Know what you do best as a business.

2 Customer focus is key.

3 Avoid increasing business risk by having all your eggs in one basket.

4 Plan to be successful!

5 Customizing the business involves every team member's efforts and ideas.

3 SYSTEMIZING
Focus, Flow, Follow

"Sometimes when you innovate, you make mistakes. It is best to admit them quickly, and get on with improving your other innovations."

STEVE JOBS

One piece of the puzzle for adding value to your business is to have documented systems and processes in place.

That point was clear when I recently spoke with an owner who had been in business several years and had experienced significant growth. She confessed that she hated walking into her branch offices and finding that not every office did things the same way.

"I want it done my way," she said. I laughed and said sometimes we have issues with letting others be accountable and responsible. We do like to have things done our way because we believe we can do it better.

She laughed and said, *"I can do it better!"*

But she realized one person cannot do it all—a shocking revelation, I know.

FACT: Having "your way" documented and clearly communicated to those who are accountable and responsible will guarantee your "better" way will be accomplished. And guess what? You reap the added benefit of eliminating some stress from your life.

As Michael Gerber states in his book *The E Myth Revisited*, "The system is the solution!" ***Every company needs to have systems in place.*** That's part of good communication and a good organization. It absolutely makes the difference in whether a business is going to succeed in the long term and whether it's going to grow.

Every important area of your business needs to be handled in a systemized way. Properly implemented systems minimize risk for you as the owner. Being able to grow the business and have systems in place is incredibly important to increase the value of your company.

Many times systems have evolved. The goal is to develop systems. Often internal business systems are focused on meeting the company's needs. But perhaps even more importantly, systems should be focused on meeting and exceeding the customers' needs. When systems are clearly communicated and followed, things run smoothly and employees are happy. Why? These employees know what they are supposed to do and how often. They know what excellence looks like!

Systemizing is not all about automation. That can and should be a component, but we are talking about systemizing your business to function well with or without you. Systemizing protects your business and helps employees focus. Systems replace your "job," as the owner, which is a vital component of reducing risk and increasing value. Too many times the business is all about the owner. This is a definite risk factor and must be addressed to get your business FIT! Any potential buyer looking to purchase a business will measure the risk. If everything is tied up with the owner and the owner is not planning to stay, risk is increased.

Reducing risk for a business includes a well functioning team of lead personalities and individuals, systems in place, and objective evidence those systems are functioning and being followed.

Owners frequently end up working 50, 60 or more hours a week because they have employees who don't know what to do or don't do what is expected on a consistent basis. The owner feels obligated to do everything. The result is the owner gets tied into the business in a way that almost guarantees it will never grow to full potential. What typically happens? You as the owner are doing everything and end up doing many of the things you do not enjoy. In other words, you're operating outside your strengths. Constantly doing the things you dislike will lead to burnout.

Another reason for systemizing is to find and retain good, qualified people. Employees want to work for companies that treat them well. They want to know what their job responsibilities are. Having systems in place satisfies that need. When you contemplate delegating some of your job responsibilities, leverage your strengths to complement the strengths of your team members. And know how to hire strategically.

A mother and her two daughters shared ownership of a business and had a system issue common in companies. I asked the mother to explain how a particular process worked. Once she responded, the daughters then said, "No, we are not doing it that way anymore." Another client had been in business for 20 years. When questioned about the company's systems, the client revealed that nothing was documented. The business had low turnover and great staff, but growth was stifled. There was no defined ideal client and no clear process for service offerings. Could the company deliver the same quality service or product to each customer?

What systems do you have? There are so many—answering the phone, billing, intakes, services or products provided are just a few of the obvious ones.

Who are the people you would like to clone in your organization? What is it they do better? What is it they say and how do they operate? If you have two billers, is there a difference between them? If one works faster, how does he do it? Does he have a unique process? This is what you want to be able to document and communicate.

You can approach systems in a couple of different ways. I suggest implementing process mapping. Bring your team together and put blank sheets of paper on the wall of your meeting room. Then take one system—customer intake, for example. Today when the phone rings, what happens?

Write down everything being said and keep asking, "and then what happens?" Document the steps and the person responsible.

You might find in working through this process that information may go back and forth between individuals; it is not a straight path. Historically, when that happens, it is because individuals have picked up parts of a former employee's job—not the entire role, just bits and pieces.

When you finish this exercise and everyone stops and reviews, ask, "Is this how we do it today? Does everyone agree?"

Then you might ask, "How can we make this easier for our customers? How can we make this easier for us? Is every step listed totally necessary? Why do we do it?"

These kinds of group discussions can be revealing. Something that runs 50 steps today could perhaps be reduced to 20.

Then review the next process, perhaps product delivery or documentation or billing. There are many, many systems that operate in a business. Once people have this awakening, they become excited about making their job and the jobs of others more logical and efficient—willing to eliminate steps they have always done without knowing or understanding why!

It's a fun, though time-consuming, project because everyone goes into the session somewhat skeptical and perhaps fearful, but comes out of it enthused because now things are going to move more smoothly, more quickly, more efficiently. Customers will be much happier. Employees will feel empowered. They know now what truly needs to be done, having addressed the process and identified the necessary steps. It's logical. The team is re-energized.

One note of caution: It will take more than one session to reach team agreement on what steps are going to change. Take time between meetings to put together the new flow chart. Then review it again. Compare the old chart with the new one. Discuss. Ask, "Have we thought of everything? Do we all agree that this will make the process easier to manage and better for the customer?"

Advantages abound for systemizing by creating work flow charts. Everyone understands how and why their responsibilities fit into the overall system. The information they are supposed to receive. Who it's coming from and the next steps in the process. They're happier because they know exactly what the expectations are.

You will be amazed when new employees see the outline. They feel confident in the company and themselves, have a shorter learning curve and increased morale. The format of the flow chart or process map can be done in a circle, straight line with arrows, whatever works best for your team.

When you develop and implement systems like this, record how much time a step should take so you'll have a benchmark for measurement. Maybe something takes a day in the beginning because of extra, inefficient steps or lack of communication and understanding of the big picture. The expectation is to get the process down to efficient, effective steps and eliminate extra, time-consuming ones.

Systems make happier owners and happier team players. Generally, employees fail to do something correctly because they do not understand *why* they are doing it. They know they are supposed to complete the action, but they don't understand why and how it fits into the big picture. Documentation helps everyone understand why it is important and how this particular system fits into the overall operation of the company.

Be sure to address different scenarios: If the answer is no, then what? If the answer is yes, then what? Work flow charts enable team members to visualize the entire process. Most people are visual learners and seeing the charts provides clarity.

Documented systems allow individuals to understand the order in which things are done. Defining responsibilities is vital. I suggest identifying the position rather than the individual person. This gives clear definition to roles and expectations of the position. ***The most important thing an owner can do is to ensure everyone knows what it is they*** *are supposed to do.* Cross train workers on the step before and after their own step in the process.

There is a tendency to pick people for cross training because their personalities are strong or some other criteria. Actually, I would suggest you look at your system and train accordingly. This way, if any person in the system leaves, is sick or takes a vacation, you have people who can step in and understand the flow of the entire system.

Please realize systemizing must occur on an ongoing basis. Regulatory changes, tax changes and system upgrades should all prompt you to ask, "How does this affect our system? What is it that we have to look at adding, subtracting, reemphasizing?" Constant review helps educate the group.

Maybe several months later you sit down and think, "So how's this working? What kind of problems have we encountered? Does it meet our needs today?"

One company identified a slow intake process for customers. There was poor communication and a disconnect between the operational and office staff. Management determined to address the problem. As they listened to everyone, someone recommended that the office staff accompany the operational staff on customer visits. This exercise revealed that the process needed to be revamped. Office workers redefined their roles to include partnering with the operational staff. This step expedited everything. Customers felt more valued and team communication improved. Forcing conversation between all key people resulted in an openness that exceeded expectations. Customer feedback improved, operational staff felt more valued as part of the team and office staff were better connected.

Participation solicited from all angles resulted in a great outcome: life made simpler. Developing awareness of what customers thought was necessary, rather than doing what the office thought was necessary, was a paradigm shift.

Strive to make it as easy as possible for customers to remain happy and satisfied while ensuring that internally you are not making yourselves totally crazy. It's not just internal feedback that you need—it is critical to have your customers' perspectives as well.

Earlier we mentioned automation as a part of systemizing. Don't overlook that piece as a means of better communication as you develop your process maps. Businesses must have systems in place to adjust workloads, improve customer focus, aid communication, visualize the big picture, improve quality of service and reduce risk. Systems prevent owner burnout and increase time capacity.

My experience over the years has led me to believe that most organizations typically fall into two general categories:

- Those that focus on the "**important** aspects" (**proactive mode**) of their business, and
- Those that are forced to focus on the "**urgent**" issues (**reactive mode**) that surface each day.

Owners from the "important" category approach their work in a deliberate and methodical manner. They see the importance of developing and implementing management systems. Systems assure a continued, unwavering focus on the most "important" aspects of the business. Then the owners can analyze the results and make adjustments accordingly.

As a result, their managers and employees have a clear understanding of the important aspects of their jobs—aspects that are reinforced every time they implement the system. Employees perform in a targeted and efficient manner every day without being sidetracked by issues that should never have surfaced in the first place!

On the other hand, owners that fall under the "urgent" category seldom find the time to focus on the "important." The absence of systems designed to focus on the "important" has put them in a never-ending cycle of dealing with the "urgent" issues that inevitably surface each day.

As a result, managers and employees lack a crystal clear understanding of the important aspects of their jobs! They are not performing in a targeted and efficient manner and are often frustrated; and, therefore, perform at an inefficient and ineffective level.

With systems in place and fully operational, the organization will begin to realize the benefits of an unwavering focus on its "important" aspects resulting in clearer communication, happier employees, better services or products and higher profit margins.

Making sure your systems are being followed and consistently reviewed becomes a constant priority. Ask questions. Involve your team. Involve your customers. Keep the process map updated and review it often with your team. Focusing on customer service and client feedback is not limited to small or large companies. It's for every company. Systemizing should create a more efficient company. But more importantly, *systemizing is about making people more efficient!* And that's what successful companies are all about!

FIT TIPS

1 Every company needs to have systems in place.

2 The most important thing an owner can do is to ensure everyone knows what it is they are supposed to do.

3 Operate in the proactive (important) rather than the reactive (urgent) mode.

4 Making sure your systems are being followed and consistently reviewed becomes a constant priority.

5 Systemizing is about making people more efficient!

4 PRIORITIZING
Build, Groom or Doom

*I've learned that people will forget what you
said, people will forget what you did, but people
will never forget how you made them feel.*

MAYA ANGELOU

People are your company's greatest asset. People are your company's greatest liability. And people are your company's greatest expense.

Prioritizing your human resources is a non-negotiable. ***People are one of the most important value drivers for any company.*** Management teams should be comprised of those people who are responsible for setting objectives, monitoring activity and motivating the "team." If your company is small, you may be the *one* person responsible for everything. But that increases risk and should be addressed.

Your team should include people with a variety of skills, typically differing from your own. Surrounding yourself with quality people is absolutely necessary for a FIT and healthy business.

Jim Collins, author of *Good to Great*, contends, "Who is more important than the What. Who comes before What." Again, highlighting the importance of people.

Prioritizing human resources is significant but often overlooked. Recruiting and turnover cost money. A conservative replacement estimate for employees making $30,000 per year or less is usually dollar for dollar. Even if 50 cents on the dollar were the figure, in this case $15,000 to replace a $30,000 per year employee, you can see how the cost adds up. The higher the position, the higher the recruiting and turnover costs. You must prioritize your human resources.

BUILD YOUR TEAM

Have you ever considered why someone would want to work for your company? This is typically insightful. When interviewing you usually focus on why you would or would not like someone to come work for your company. Seldom do you ask them why they would want to come work for your company. What do they know about your company? Do you and your team believe it is a great place to work?

Can you connect employee activity to company success? Few owners can give a convincing "Yes!" Have you regularly and directly communicated to each of your employees the importance of their role to the success of the company?

When employees don't understand their specific purpose, they are easily frustrated, often lack motivation and are not terribly efficient in their activities. From a value and risk perspective, this is not good!

By clearly defining your expectations for each position, you will be able to hire more effectively based on the strengths needed for the role. When people operate within their strengths, they are going to treat customers better, achieve more on a daily basis and have more positive and creative moments!

Additionally, understanding personality types, yours and others', will affect how you act, react, and make decisions. Your primary style can tell you a great deal about how you are motivated, environments you prefer, your greatest fears, how you communicate and how you prefer others to communicate with you. Understanding how to determine another's preferred behavior style is the key to unlocking better communication.

According to *Harvard Business Review*, "the number one criterion for advancement and promotion for professionals is an ability to communicate effectively." And, of course, the reverse is equally true—one of the biggest reasons leaders fail is their *inability* to communicate.

Without meaningful communication, prioritizing human resources will be significantly hindered. Trying to communicate with people whose communication style is different from yours can be challenging—especially if you haven't learned to recognize and appreciate these differences. You become frustrated and are likely to react negatively. Awareness of another's motivations can allow you to identify and diffuse problems before they even start.

Building a solid infrastructure requires an appreciation of the different perspectives others contribute to the team. The tendency to hire people very similar to yourself is not always good idea.

Your team needs diverse personalities, skills, experiences and strengths. People are unique. Realizing and appreciating different personalities and strengths gives you the ability to gain credibility and positively influence others.

If you *are* your business, there is little likelihood a buyer will find your company valuable. The most valuable businesses are those for which the owner is not critical to its ongoing success. Buyers are hesitant to purchase a company whose owner possesses all the knowledge, skills and relationships.

Many owners cling to the critical marketing and sales activities. They worry that employees responsible for these tasks will fail. While it can be difficult to find and hire the right employees, your ability to teach and trust your marketing and sales staff is critical to building value in your company. You can't carry this burden alone. Your experience and skills generate much more value when you are the mentor for employees.

Build a solid management team and groom a successor. You need to have systems and processes as we have discussed, but people run those systems. Your business cannot generate revenue without people. If the business is only you, that presents a huge risk to a potential buyer. When you are gone, what happens to the business? If you handle marketing and sales, you have all the connections and relationships. You are passionate about your business but at some point you must migrate from the role of employee to mentor, becoming the coach of your team.

Know what you do best and what you don't. Operate from your strengths and create an environment that ensures your team does the same. Operate with the mantra "You cannot be anything you want to be—but you can be a lot more of who you already are." Tom Rath, *Strengths Finder 2.0*

GROOM OR DOOM

Have you ever worked at a company where an underperforming person was never reprimanded and the problem never addressed, much less resolved? The negative impact on other employees and the company can be devastating. In an organization I am familiar with, one senior vice president had a disagreement with the CEO. Rather than confronting and resolving the issue, the CEO "asked" the senior VP to move to the next floor down! Now, do you think this was an effective way to remedy the situation? Undoubtedly, the manner in which this issue was handled (or lack thereof) negatively impacted other departments of the organization.

Are you willing to have those tough conversations with current employees? I love this quote by Peter Drucker: "Executives owe it to the organization and to their fellow workers not to tolerate non-performing individuals in important jobs." Do you have positions that are *not* important? Let's hope not.

Ignoring employee performance issues will cost you money. How?

- Employee turnover—losing higher performers because low performance has no consequence.
- Inefficient and less effective time management.
- Loss of customers and business due to poor service provided by poor performance.

One company leader shared an incident he had with a known low performer "out of control." I insisted he needed to deal with this employee. "Well, I don't have time," he replied. Several weeks later, he began receiving calls from unhappy employees and disgruntled customers threatening to move business elsewhere. The situation had escalated, and became a priority. Now he had to *make* time to deal with the performance issues! (See Step 3, "Systemizing," Important vs. Urgent)

Companies typically have a mix of high, mid- and low performers. High performers thrive on achievement. They have high expectations for themselves and expect the same from the organization.

Mid-performers make up a sizeable majority of any workforce. The main difference between high and mid-performers is consistency—or I could say inconsistency.

Low performers left unattended drag down mid-performers, drive high performers out the door and take up a large percentage of the manager's time. All of which has a price tag. None of us will be 100 percent all the time on our hires. But stop to consider—how much did your last bad hire cost?

Promptly addressing performance issues has benefits:

- Retaining high achievers
- Encouraging mid-performers to be consistent
- Adding $$$ to your bottom line.

One other aspect of prioritizing human resources is addressing how business owners take care of themselves. One owner shared that after 20 years of running her business, she woke up one morning hating it. She didn't want to go to work anymore and didn't feel she was serving her vendors or her customers. She had been pedaling so hard for so many years, and this day she woke up and had crashed into a wall. She no longer felt fulfilled and realized she had neglected to take care of herself. Her identity was so wrapped up in the business she had to unravel from it.

She had no plan for her exit, and now was forced to make a reactive rather than proactive decision. She decided to pursue a sale. As she began the process, problems were unearthed—with contracts and with the management team. *Risk* for the buyer! What did she decide to do about it? Nothing! She decided to do nothing. *(#FIT TIP Chapter 1 item 3—Indecision is the wrong decision!)*

She loved her managers but they were not doing their jobs. Unwilling to have the tough conversations, she decided to make the management team the next person's problem. She ended up selling the business to a less-than-ideal buyer who offered her asking price but asked her to carry an unsecured note for a significant portion. *Risk* for the seller. One by one employees and vendors started to leave. Within three years the buyer defaulted on the note and the company went bankrupt, leaving the seller with a $500,000 loss.*

Take care of yourself. If you do not have the right people in the right positions, take immediate steps to remedy the situation. They will drain you and the rest of your team. Take your losses and don't be afraid to have the hard conversations.

GROOM	DOOM
Surround yourself with the right people	*Underachievers affect your team*

---

* Please note, this seller entered the market alone without any advisory representation.

GROOM	DOOM
Empower people to use their strengths	*Negativity spreads like a cancer*
Proactive Communication	*Reactive Communication*

Leaders empower people. Have confidence in your team and be willing to step aside and let them use their talents. You cannot do everything.

- Hire people to do the things you don't do well.
- Be involved.
- Have a process.
- Prioritize your human resources—your biggest asset, your biggest liability, your biggest expense. You can't afford not to.

FIT TIPS

1 People are one of the most important value drivers for any company.

2 Build a solid management team and groom a successor.

3 Have those tough conversations with employees.

4 Ignoring employee performance issues will cost you money.

5 Low performers left unattended drag down mid-performers.

5 ANALYZING
Conquering Costs and Consequences

"Business, more than any other occupation, is a continual dealing with the future; it is a continual calculation, an instinctive exercise in foresight."

HENRY R. LUCE

Your financials tell a story about your business. ***Do you know your financial story?***

Analyzing your financials is imperative. It can also be intimidating. *But* don't let that keep you from asking—and getting answers to—your questions! *Please* don't choose to ignore the financial analysis piece of the puzzle in your business. It *will* have detrimental consequences.

You may not be an accountant or numbers person. That's all right. Not everyone has this skill set. Simply search out a qualified and trusted person to add to your team of advisors.

I worked with a business owner a few years ago who assumed she would keep her business and pass it down to her family. She never considered selling. The co-owner (also a family member) always had the thought in the back of his mind that even if they were not going to consider selling, they should at least understand what the market was like out there—what was happening and what people were doing.

He took the initiative to have conversations with people like me to be educated on the industry market.

One day in the midst of dealing with debt and stress, the founder told the co-owner she had decided to sell and retire! They quickly discovered that they couldn't just say, "OK, let's sell." They had not and were not prepared.

They realized they didn't know the critical numbers necessary to have conversations with buyers. They began a concerted focus to learn their financial story, regretting that they had not begun the planning process a few years earlier. It is important to have a good two or three years of solid performance before thinking about selling.

One lesson learned—even if you are adamant about not selling, at least work on your margins and get your business FIT. If you decide at the last minute to sell, all that work and preparation is done.

Starting sooner is a key issue. The process is not quick. The ideal in this situation would have been to have a couple of years to prepare. But even in six months they found ways to save money and make the business more profitable.

One good financial motto should be ***manage the margins***. It is extremely beneficial to have a qualified person from the outside looking in, along with you as the owner looking from the inside out. The two perspectives combined are powerful.

In this instance, they did not know what their gross margin was or what it should have been. The gross margin is the difference between what you can bill or collect and what you have to pay for the product or service. They discovered they had been running approximately 10 percent lower than industry standard. What an eye opener! That immediately gave some clarity to the financial struggles they were experiencing.

They quickly implemented a few simple cost-saving measures. They reduced some of their travel reimbursements, adjusted some pay rates, focused on decreasing overtime and a few other items. Their gross margins improved over the next six months.

Simultaneously, they looked at their operational expenses. These are defined as expenses for which you cannot bill, i.e. administrative costs, rent, utilities, phones, marketing, etc. We discovered they were administratively overstaffed. They hired a time-management firm, and as a result of that study, they combined several administrative positions— yielding a cost savings of 4 percent. This was a definite positive for the company both financially and for employee efficiency and effectiveness.

Reviewing revenue sources was also insightful. They discovered there were certain lines of business that were actually losing money. They made the tough decision to no longer pursue those services. Rather, priority focus was placed on the other service lines that were more profitable.

They used the industry benchmarks I provided to determine where they needed to be. They did their analysis internally, made changes and began running a leaner business. Their financial story was improving.

Next, they started to do projections based on their changes, and could now see how the future would look based on their current performance. With this data, they understood why it would have been better to plan ahead. They also realized they could have been more profitable over those previous years. They were excited about moving in the right direction.

What kept them from starting sooner? Part of it was a hesitation to commit to selling. Realize you are not committing to a sale, but committing to get your business healthier and FIT to have the option to sell if you want to.

Sometimes it is difficult to differentiate between the two—a healthy business vs. a business you plan to sell. It is hard to think about the long-term plan because of your emotional attachment to the business. It's hard to work *on* the business rather than just *for* the business. Many owners start at ground zero. The emotional attachment is real! It's difficult to sell your "baby."

Approaching from the standpoint of getting your business healthier is a great first step. It provides options for business owners. *Tracking the value of your business from year to year* is invaluable. Profitability and value give you leverage as an owner.

At the end of the day, if you decide you don't want to sell, you don't have to! Consider the story of CLIF Bar. Gary Erickson, a baker and former mountain guide, got the idea for his product in 1990 on a daylong, 175-mile bike ride, for which he packed a variety of energy bars. Two years later after experimenting in his mother's kitchen, he settled on a recipe for what would become the CLIF Bar. Sales doubled each year, and by 1997, revenue surpassed $20 million. In April 2000, Erickson turned down a $120 million offer from Quaker Oats to buy the company. *A healthy business means a healthy bottom line.* There are no downsides!

Many times business owners view the business as an extension of who they are. Answering the question "What's next, if I don't do this, what will I do?" can be tough. Planning ahead and knowing what other passions and interests you have can make all the difference.

In the instance of our co-owners, upon the successful sale of their business, one owner retired and is now busier than ever volunteering, taking computer classes, spending time with grandchildren and having fun. The other took a position with the purchasing company. He never thought he would take that path because they were friendly competitors. However, they made a great connection and balanced each other well. Business lines, philosophy, mission and vision were all aligned. It just made sense. He felt respected, liked and appreciated and continues to add value to the new organization. Both the buyer and the seller believe the transaction and the transition went better than either could have imagined. I love happy endings!

One component to a successful transaction is trust, which needs to be established between the buyer and seller. Obviously, it lessens the buyer's risk when a trusting seller wants to see the company continue to grow and move ahead. Trust reduces risk for the seller as well, and builds confidence and support for the business to move forward.

Starting, growing and maintaining a healthy business is hard work! And all that effort and energy should be focused on building a healthy rather than an unhealthy business. Knowing your financial story requires asking and answering unlimited questions. Your profit is in the details. *Paying attention to financial details is the difference between growing a healthy or an unhealthy business.* We have talked about gross margins, revenue, bottom line profit, projections, administrative costs, profitable vs. unprofitable business lines. These are just a few of the areas to examine.

Many business owners grow their top-line revenue by adding additional services. But a detailed analysis reveals these additional services are not contributing to an increase in the bottom line profit. You must monitor growth of revenue/sales (top line) as well as growth of profit (bottom line).

It's a waste of your time and energy to grow sales and make no profit.

Business leases are another expense that warrants monitoring. They can be a big profit gobbler. If you are in the start-up phase, it can be a substantial risk to sign a long-term lease (five to ten years).

Growing business value hinges primarily on risk perception. If your business is perceived as having considerable risk, the value decreases. If on the other hand your business is perceived as low-risk, value increases. Much of this risk perception hinges on your financial story.

Other financial areas to review would be your billing process and how quickly you receive payment for your products or services. Do you have high risk of non-payment? Are there considerable write-offs or collection issues?

Diversification of revenue sources is another piece of your financial story. Do most of your sales come from one or two sources? What would happen to you and your business if that source went elsewhere? I informed one business owner that the business was high-risk for this very reason. I advised the owner to diversify the funding source and recommended hiring a person for sales and marketing. The owner agreed. Within two weeks of our conversation, the primary revenue source had a funding cut. This was a painful point of transition! I am happy to say, however, the owners did work through this painful transition and continue to flourish and grow.

Do you have ongoing marketing efforts? Can those efforts be tracked and measured? Are those efforts all yours as the owner or diversified with a sales team?

Questions, questions, questions! Knowing the right questions to ask and getting answers to those questions is the way to create your successful financial story.

Whether your plan is to keep the business for passive income, or gift to children, or sell it to a third party, *risk* is the ultimate factor that drives value either up or down. Asking and getting answers to your financial questions is key. If you don't know what questions to ask, you definitely will not get the right answers. Take time to find trusted financial and industry advisors to help and encourage you along the journey to building and growing a financially FIT business.

Don't wait! Prepare now!

FIT TIPS

1 Know your financial story.

2 Manage the margins.

3 Track the value of your business from year to year.

4 A healthy business means a healthy bottom line.

5 Attention to financial details makes the difference between growing a healthy or an unhealthy business.

CONCLUSION

*"If one does not know to which port one
is sailing, no wind is favorable."*

LUCIUS ANNAEUS SENECA

So where are you heading? Please don't confuse building a big company with building a valuable one. How FIT is your business? Where do you need to make changes to increase value and decrease risk? Where are you in the process of creating a business that has real value and doesn't just "pay the bills?" Do you have a plan? Do you have good people? Is your company profitable?

Reviewing our 5 Steps:

1. **Organizing**—Know and be *clear about your goals*.
2. **Customizing**—Know *why* what you do is valuable.
3. **Systemizing**—Know *how* you do it and document it.

4. **Prioritizing**—Know *what* strengths are needed for each position. *Focus on profitable hires.*
5. **Analyzing**—Know *how* to create value in your business.

Growing a FIT business requires you to be proactive, working *on* your business, not just *for* your business, increasing value and decreasing risk.

As I mentioned in the introduction, waves of upcoming owners wishing to sell are on the horizon. The challenge is to be intentional with your planning and preparation for the transition *before* you want out. *5 Steps to Get Your Business FIT and ready to go when you are* is a tool to be used to help create awareness and motivate you to be proactive and *get your business FIT.*

My mission is to help *Get Your Business FIT and ready to go when you are.* Most owners have a good bit, if not all, of their life's savings tied up in their business. You want to have something to show for a lifetime of work. You don't want to realize too late that your company has no value because one customer makes up too much revenue or you are too dependent on one supplier or one key employee or any of a number of high-risk factors.

You may or may not be years away from selling. Start *planning NOW.* You will be able to create much more value. And creating a FIT company now makes running your business more fun along the way, less stressful and more profitable. You have the winning hand. When you are ready to sell, you can sell for a premium price and control the negotiation because *you have options*. Buyers are always looking to purchase FIT companies! Make your efforts count. Build an organization into a success story.

FIT TIPS
SUMMARY GUIDE

INTRODUCTION

1. Planning for the unexpected requires focus on being prepared, open and ready to take advantage of the future.
2. There is always a market for FIT, healthy businesses.
3. Identifying the business goals that are most important to you will help ensure they are met.
4. The goal of planning ahead is to focus on your objectives.

GETTING STARTED: 3 NO'S TO KNOW

1. The goal is to increase value and decrease risk.
2. Passively choosing "no plan" is a decision to settle for the least profitable exit for yourself and your family.
3. One of the most important value drivers in any business is its management team.
4. One of the first questions a prospective buyer will ask is, "Who runs the company and are they willing to stay?
5. Don't assume your staff understands the business as you do.

CHAPTER 1: ORGANIZING—STRUCTURES, SET-UPS AND SHARES

1. Know and understand your entity structure.
2. If you currently have partners and you DO NOT have a buy-sell agreement, PLEASE, PLEASE GET ONE.
3. Avoid setting up partnerships with all partners having equal shares.
4. Review the buy-sell agreement at least once per year.

CHAPTER 2: CUSTOMIZING—BEST, GOOD, RETHINK

1. Know what you do best as a business.
2. Customer focus is key.
3. Avoid increasing business risk by having all your eggs in one basket.
4. Plan to be successful!
5. Customizing the business involves every team member's efforts and ideas.

CHAPTER 3: SYSTEMIZING—FOCUS, FLOW, FOLLOW

1. Every company needs to have systems in place.
2. The most important thing an owner can do is to ensure everyone knows what it is they are supposed to do.
3. Operate in the proactive (important) rather than the reactive (urgent) mode.

4. Making sure your systems are being followed and consistently reviewed becomes a constant priority.
5. Systemizing is about making people more efficient!

CHAPTER 4: PRIORITIZING—BUILD, GROOM OR DOOM

1. People are one of the most important value drivers for any company.
2. Build a solid management team and groom a successor.
3. Have those tough conversations with employees.
4. Ignoring employee performance issues will cost you money.
5. Low performers left unattended drag down mid-performers.

CHAPTER 5: ANALYZING—CONQUERING COSTS AND CONSEQUENCES

1. Know your financial story.
2. Manage the margins.
3. Track the value of your business from year to year.
4. A healthy business means a healthy bottom line.
5. Attention to financial details makes the difference between growing a healthy or unhealthy business.

ABOUT THE AUTHOR

Risa Baker is founder and managing director of Partners 31, a business coaching and advisory firm. She is an M&A advisor, Certified Life Coach, author, speaker, business owner, wife, mother, grandmother, life-long learner, people-lover.

She has brokered and assisted with over $100 million in acquisitions and transactions.

The opportunity to oversee and turnaround a multi-faceted agency was her entrance into the home health and human service industries.

As director of development for a large corporation, she was responsible for targeting companies for acquisition throughout the United States, assessing valuation, financial analysis, and operational feasibility.

These life experiences have provided a unique privilege to work with a variety of business owners and companies. Sharing her expertise with others is her passion. She brings a definite energy and vitality to whatever she tackles and truly enjoys facilitation of transformation!

Building relationships with her clients is key to achieving client-focused objectives and working to *Get Your Business FIT and ready to go when you are.*

TAKE THE NEXT STEP!

COACHING, SEMINARS, INTERIM SUPPORT

What is your next step? Knowing what actions to take comes from having clarity. Get the clarity you need by having a Partners 31 *Coach in your Corner*. Our next-step options help you move forward in your resolve to have a FIT business include:

- ✓ **Assessment**
- ✓ Ongoing **Coaching**
- ✓ One or multi-day on-site **Seminars**
- ✓ On-site **development and operational interim support**
- ✓ **Buyer and Seller Representation**

Put our team and expertise to work for you! For more information contact us at **info@partners31.com**.

SPEAKING

I frequently speak about selling and buying businesses, planning to be successful, personal development and team development. For more information on keynotes and workshops, please email **risa@partners31.com**.

Do you know business owners or organizations that would benefit from reading

5 Steps to Get Your Business FIT?

We offer bulk discount rates on orders of 50 or more.

Please contact us at **info@partners31.com** for discount pricing

www.ingramcontent.com/pod-product-compliance
Lightning Source LLC
Chambersburg PA
CBHW070944210326
41520CB00021B/7043